Adam the Ant's Polka Dot Pants
Written and Illustrated by
Lori Kaiser

Another great book in the Xavier Series!

Published by
Carpe Diem Publishers
17401 Betty Blvd.
Canyon, TX 79015
806-433-6321

www.carpediempublishers.com

© Copyright, 2010 by Carpe Diem Publishers. All Rights Reserved. No portion of this book may be reproduced, stored in a retrieval system, or transmitted, in any form or by any means, electronic, mechanical, photocopying, recording, or otherwise without prior written permission from publisher.
Printed in the United States of America
ISBN 978-0-9845761-0-4

Adam the Ant's Polka Dot Pants

and everyone thought they were keen.

but Adam was one of the nicer ants.

Zane the zebra had a dream.

the teacher called on Max to read the next line.

Zane the zebra had a dream.

so THEY began to taunt and tease!

Zane the zebra had a dream.

"Max is a bully we know this is true, but he needs our help 'cause he's lonely and blue."

That was the day a new friendship was born. Adam taught Max to read and write on the board.

He also taught Max how a person should be: To love the Lord, your friends, and your enemies.

www.ingramcontent.com/pod-product-compliance
Lightning Source LLC
Chambersburg PA
CBHW042045290426
44109CB00001B/37